SAINT SAYINGS
about
Hope

Illustrated by Beth Ann Ramos

For my boys. I will always love you more
than the world.

~Mom

The quotes in this book were gathered from multiple
sources and are presented as they were previously
quoted. Effort has been made to ensure their
accuracy, but the Publisher cannot guarantee their
perfect accuracy.

Illustrated by Beth Ann Ramos
Published by Good Day Books
First Edition

Learn more at www.bethannramos.com.

good day
BOOKS

A Gift For:

_____

Isaiah 40:31

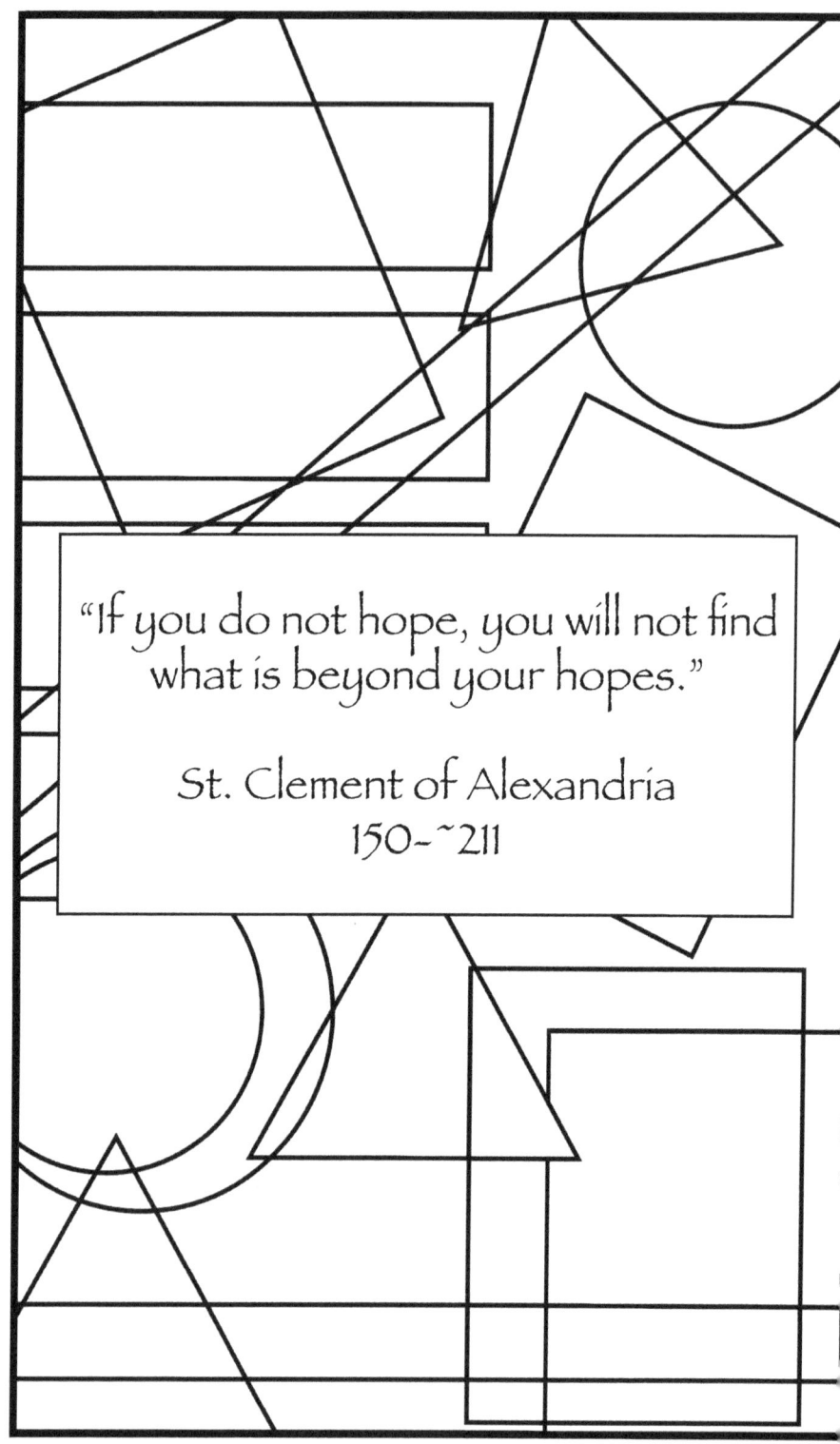

"If you do not hope, you will not find what is beyond your hopes."

St. Clement of Alexandria
150-~211

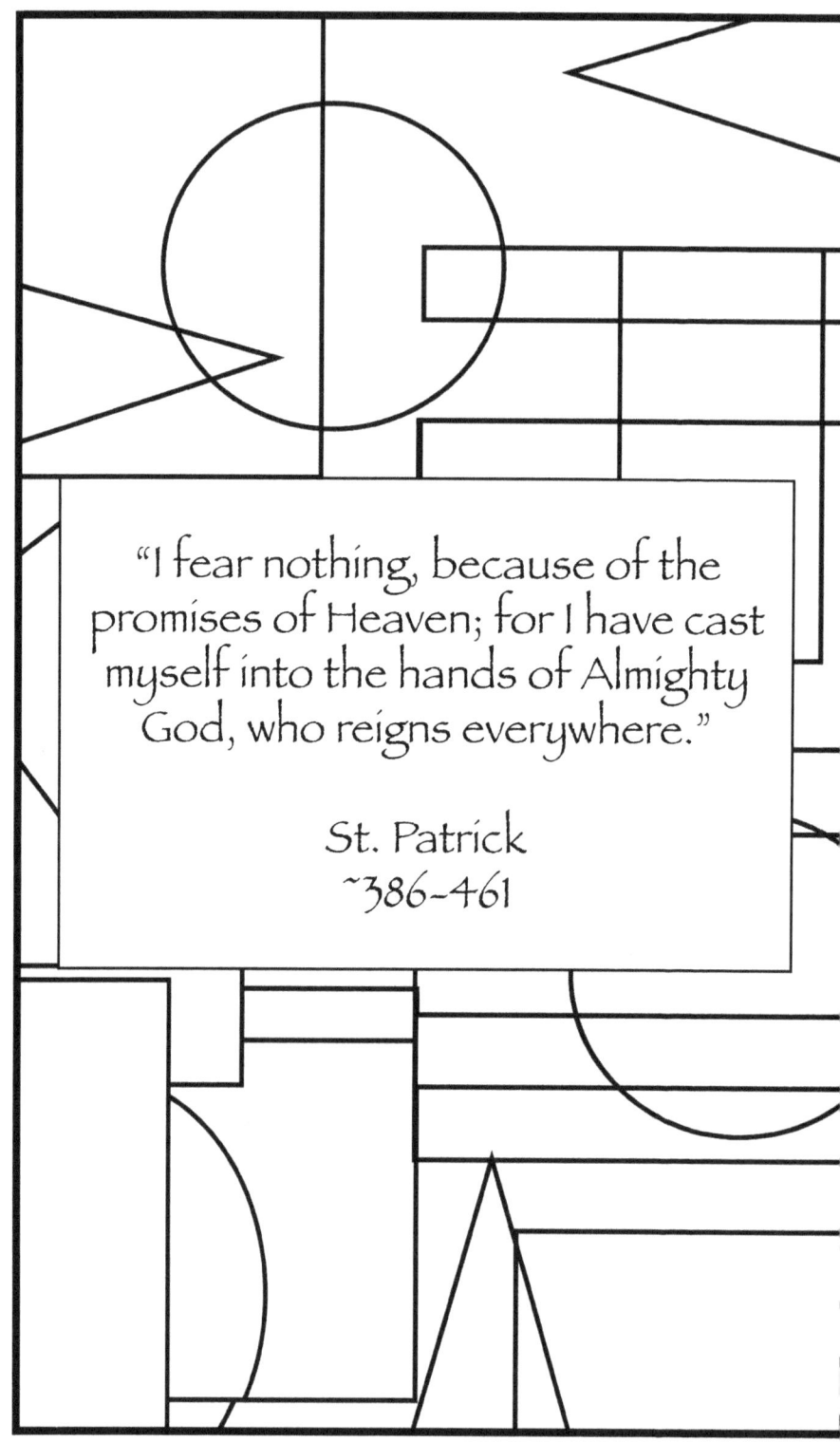

"I fear nothing, because of the promises of Heaven; for I have cast myself into the hands of Almighty God, who reigns everywhere."

St. Patrick
~386-461

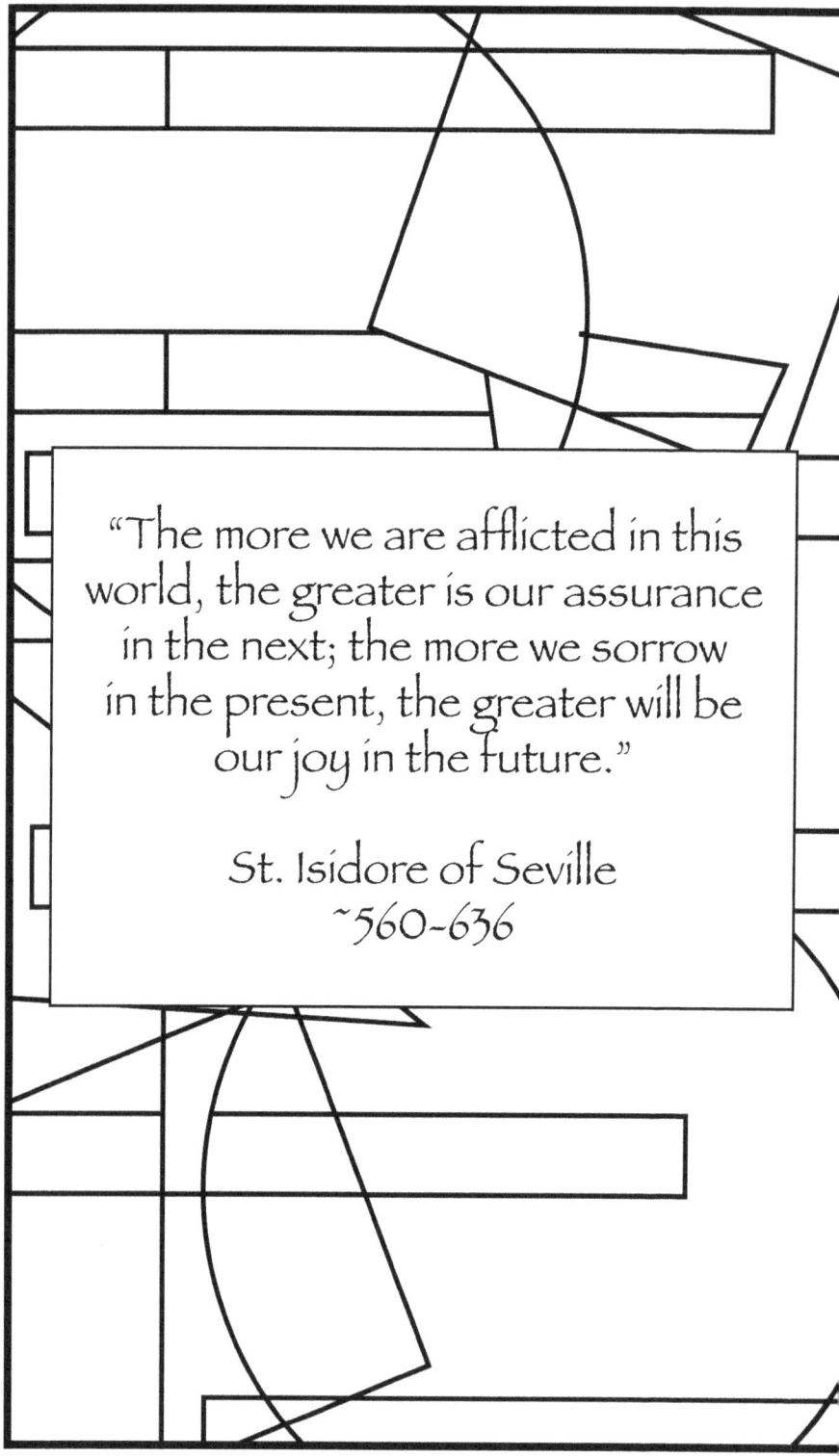

"The more we are afflicted in this world, the greater is our assurance in the next; the more we sorrow in the present, the greater will be our joy in the future."

St. Isidore of Seville
~560-636

"All the darkness in the world cannot extinguish the light of a single candle."

St. Francis of Assisi
1181~1226

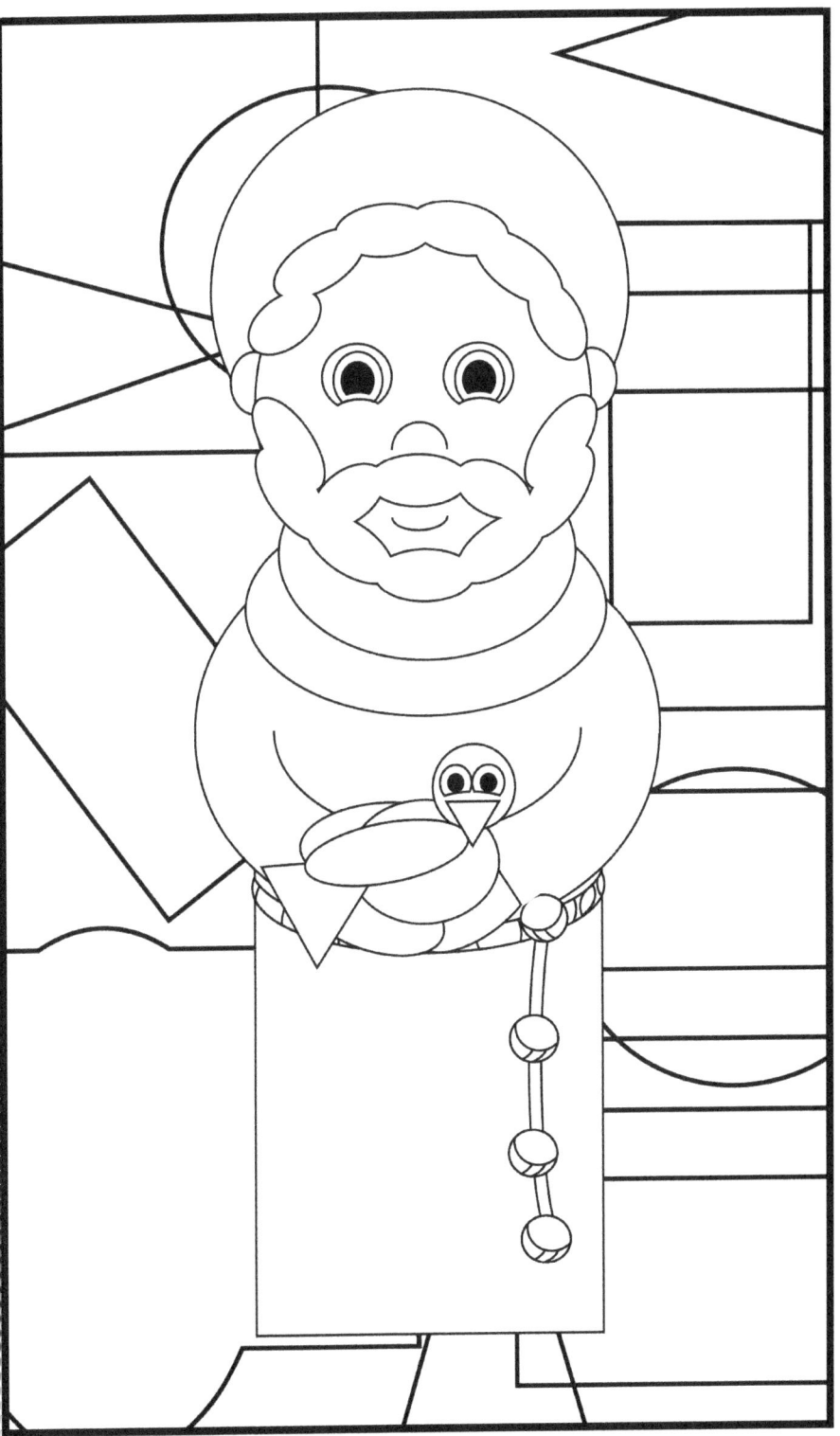

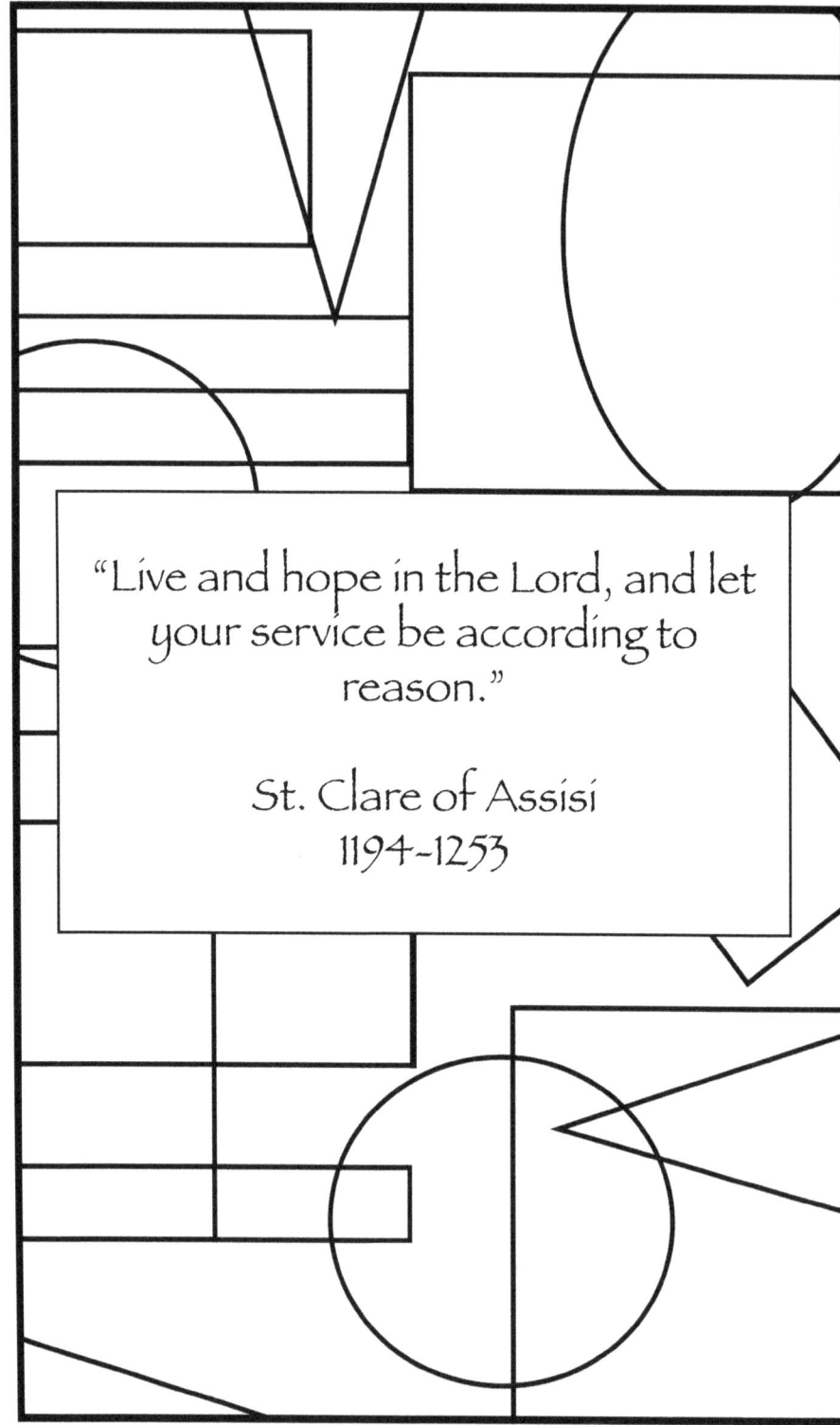

"Live and hope in the Lord, and let your service be according to reason."

St. Clare of Assisi
1194-1253

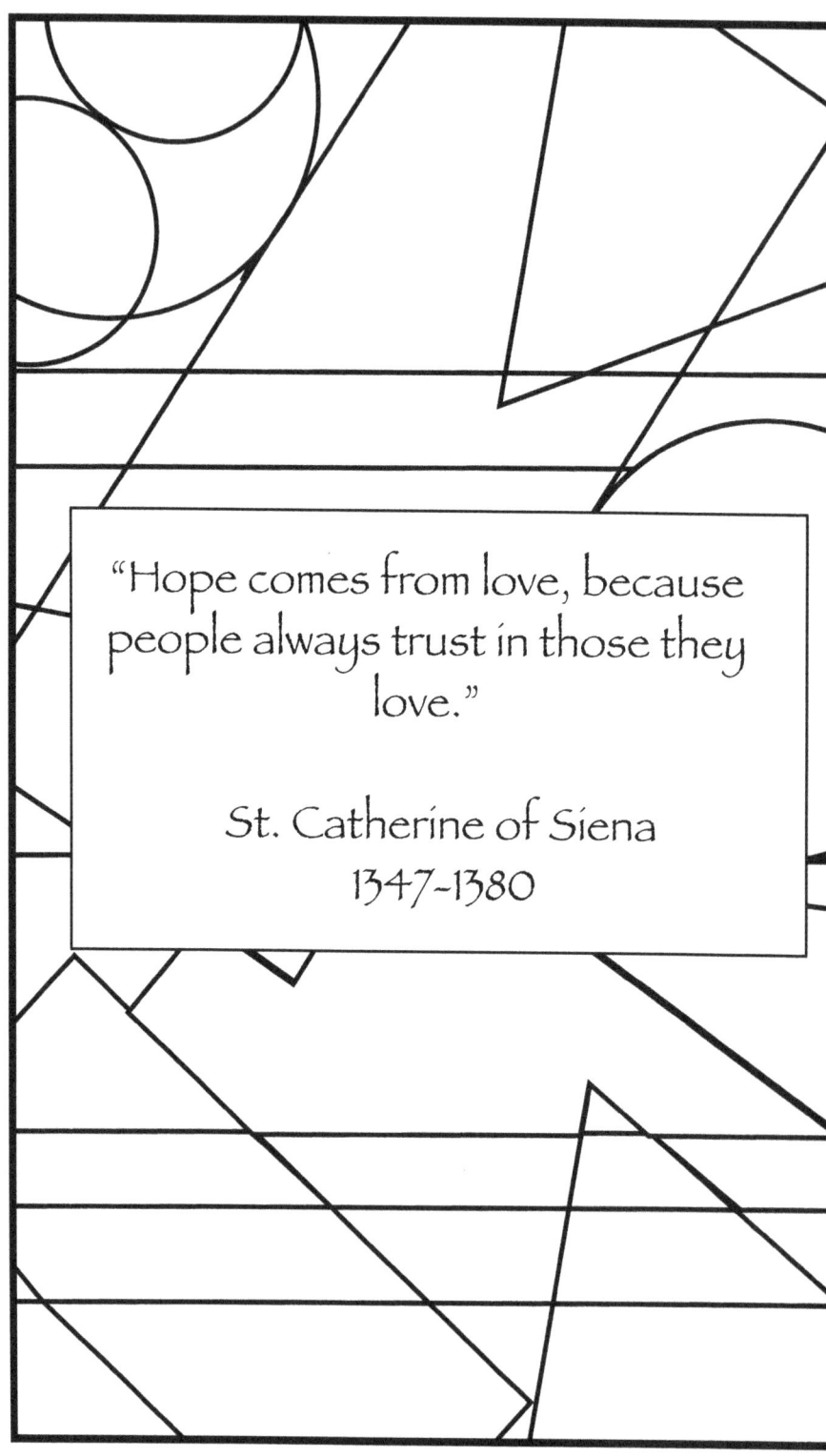

"Hope comes from love, because people always trust in those they love."

St. Catherine of Siena
1347–1380

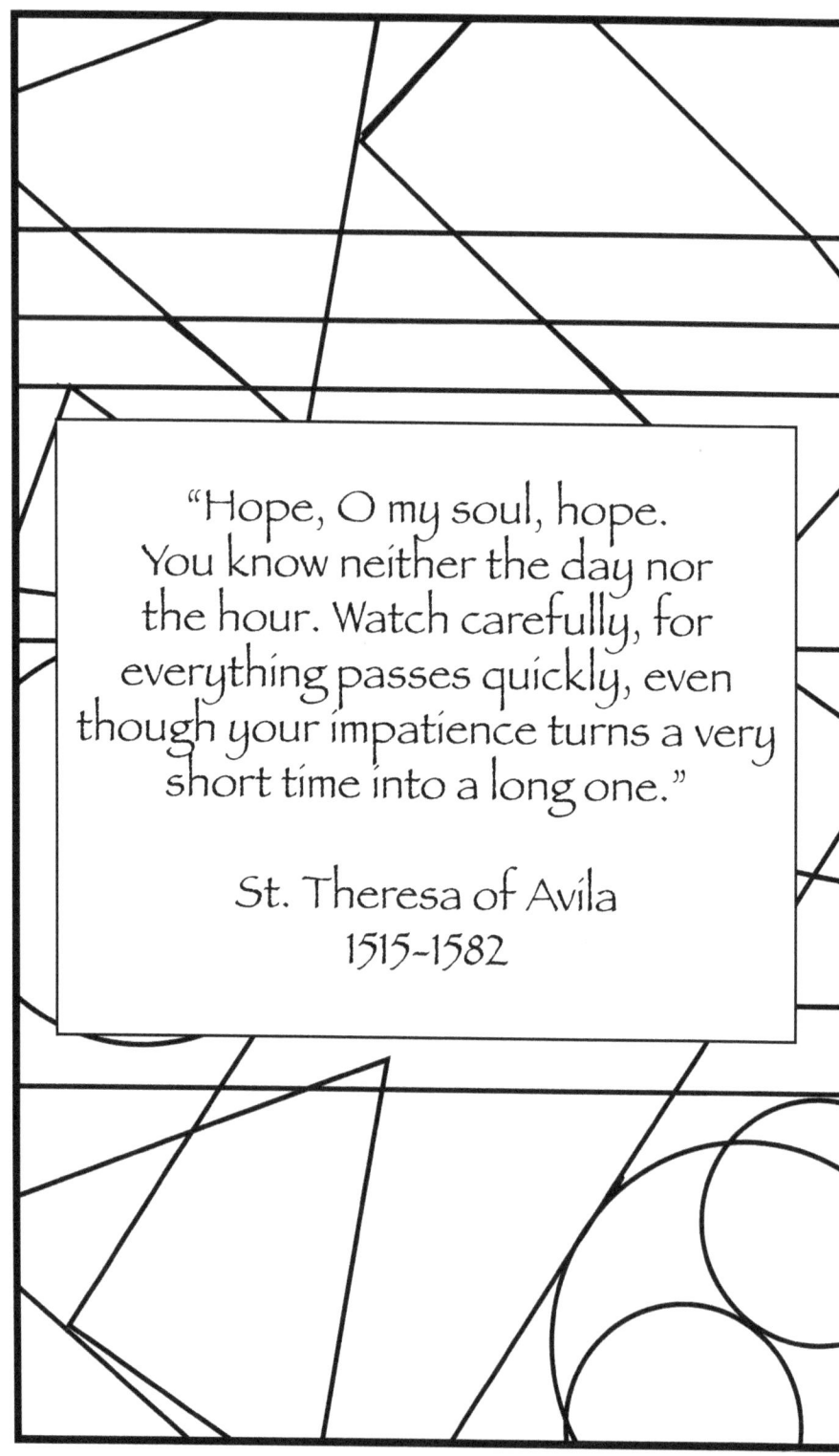

"Hope, O my soul, hope.
You know neither the day nor
the hour. Watch carefully, for
everything passes quickly, even
though your impatience turns a very
short time into a long one."

St. Theresa of Avila
1515-1582

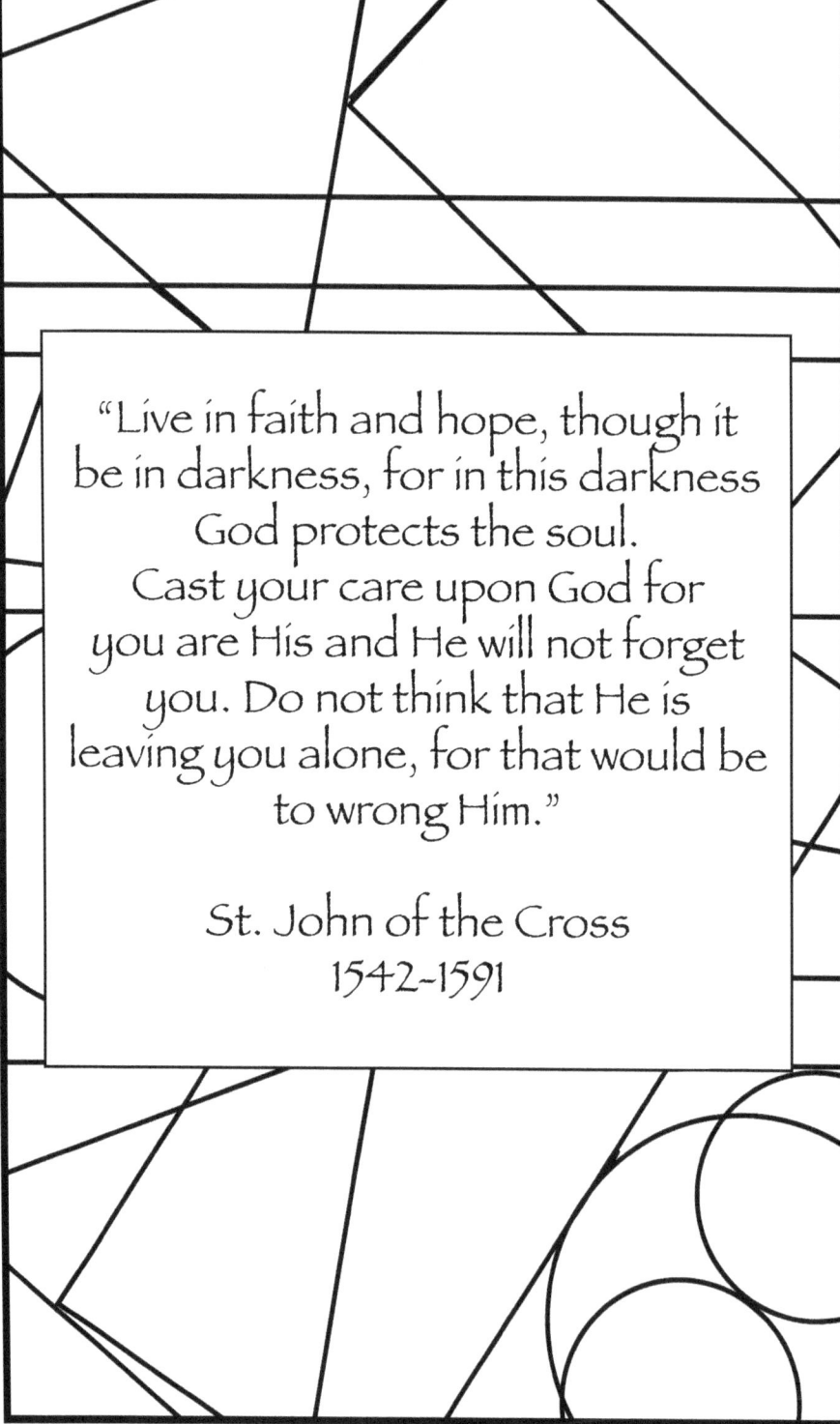

"Live in faith and hope, though it be in darkness, for in this darkness God protects the soul.
Cast your care upon God for you are His and He will not forget you. Do not think that He is leaving you alone, for that would be to wrong Him."

St. John of the Cross
1542-1591

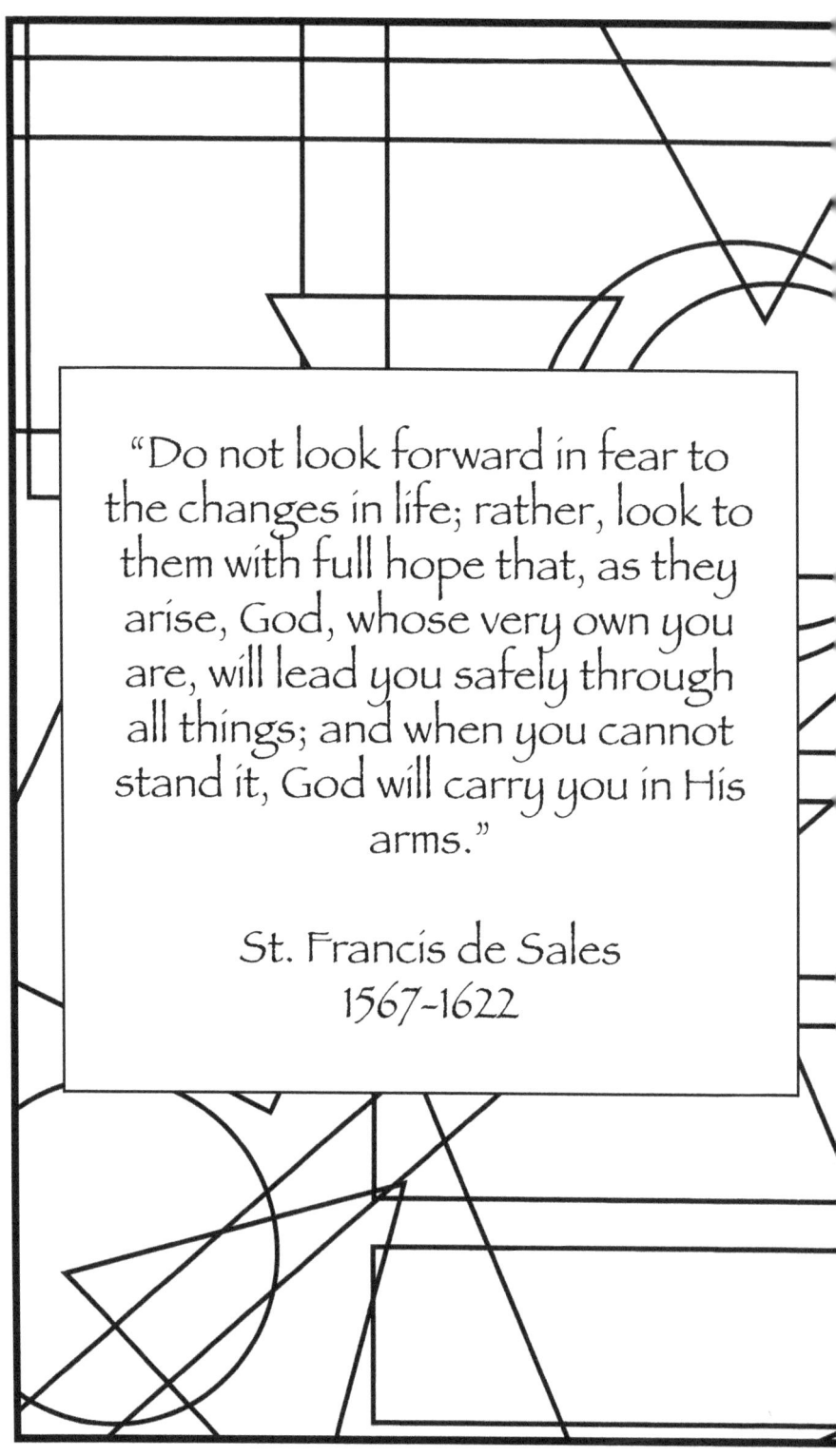

"Do not look forward in fear to the changes in life; rather, look to them with full hope that, as they arise, God, whose very own you are, will lead you safely through all things; and when you cannot stand it, God will carry you in His arms."

St. Francis de Sales
1567–1622

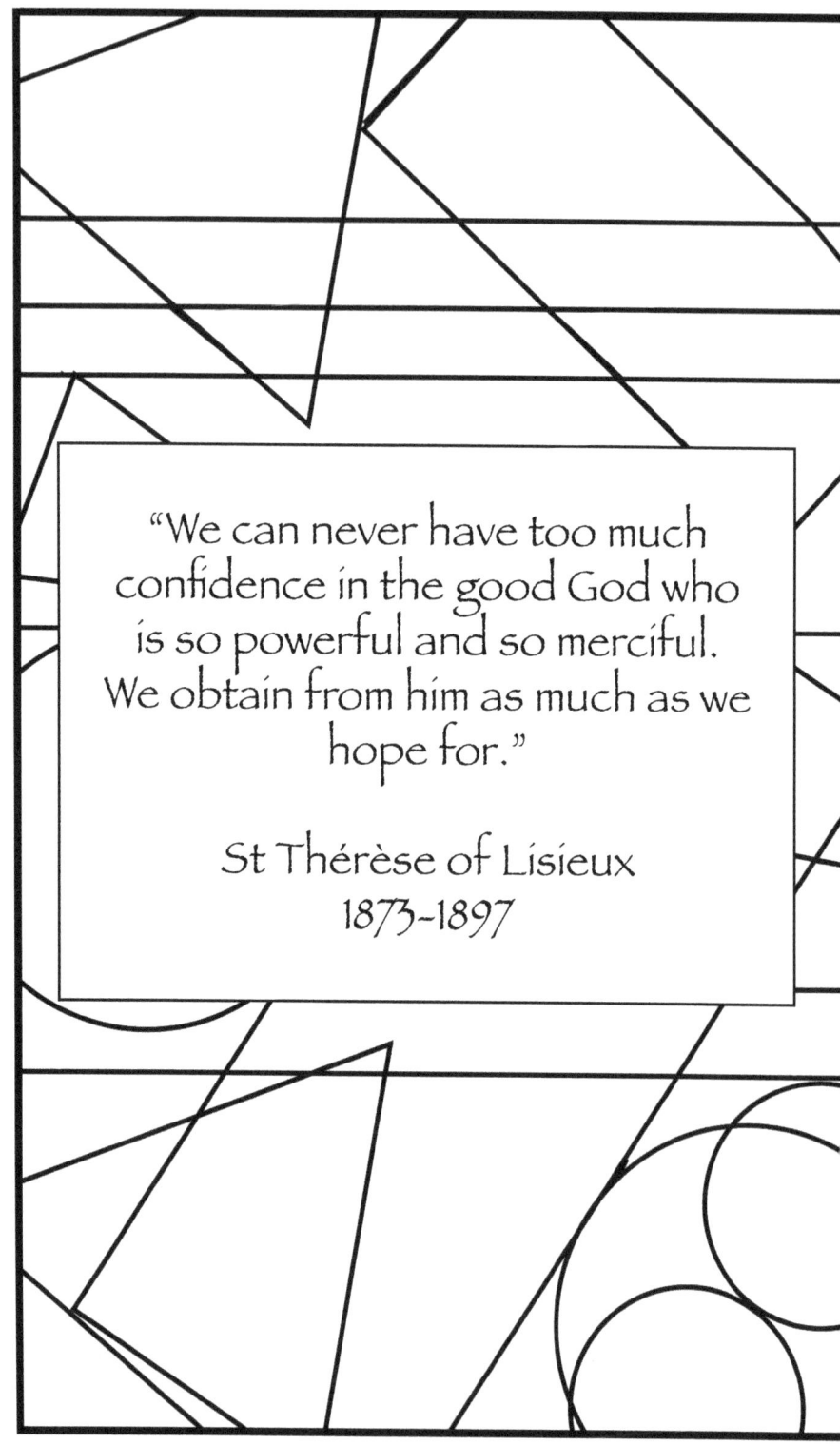

"We can never have too much confidence in the good God who is so powerful and so merciful. We obtain from him as much as we hope for."

St Thérèse of Lisieux
1873-1897

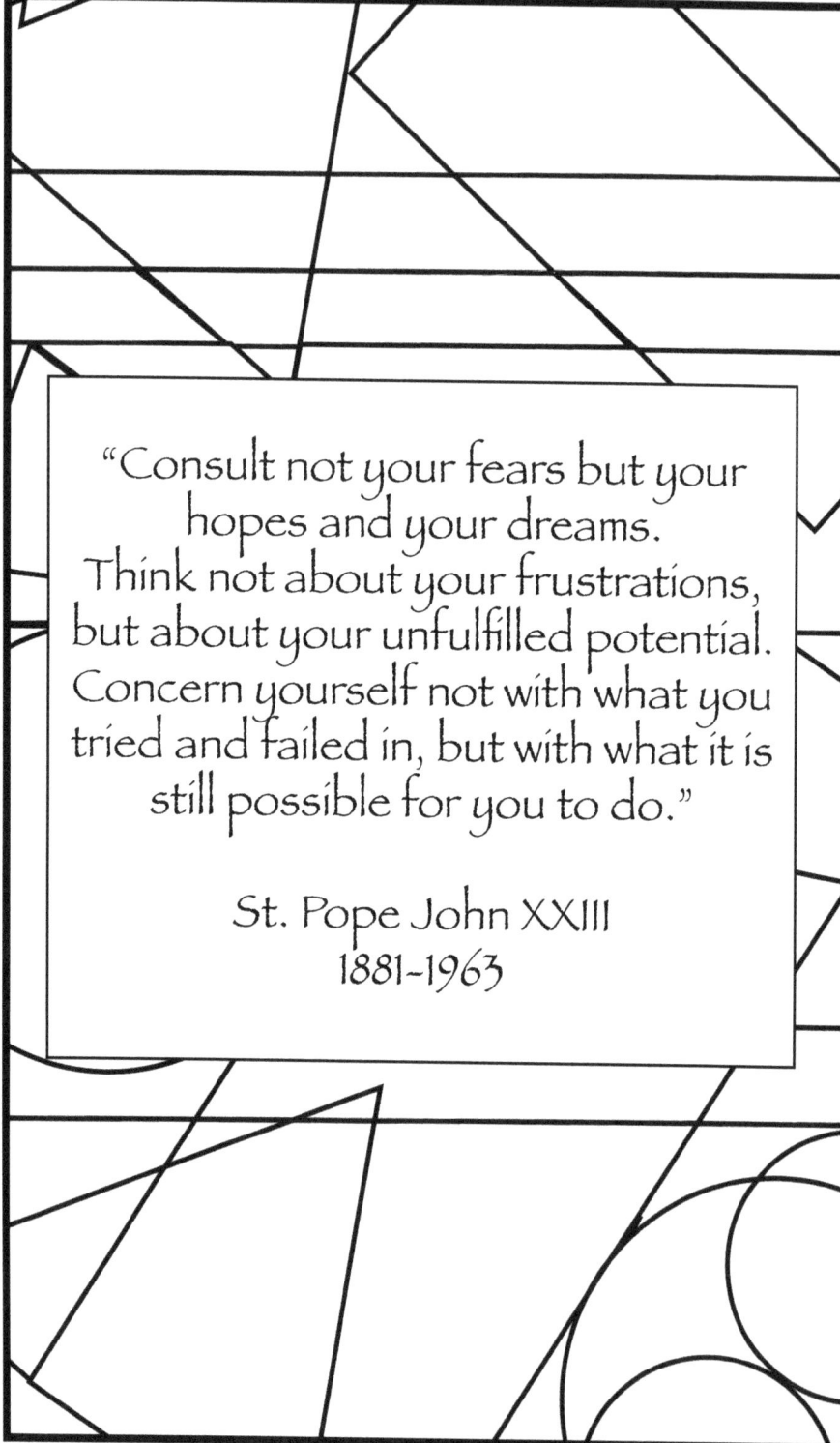

"Consult not your fears but your hopes and your dreams.
Think not about your frustrations, but about your unfulfilled potential.
Concern yourself not with what you tried and failed in, but with what it is still possible for you to do."

St. Pope John XXIII
1881-1963

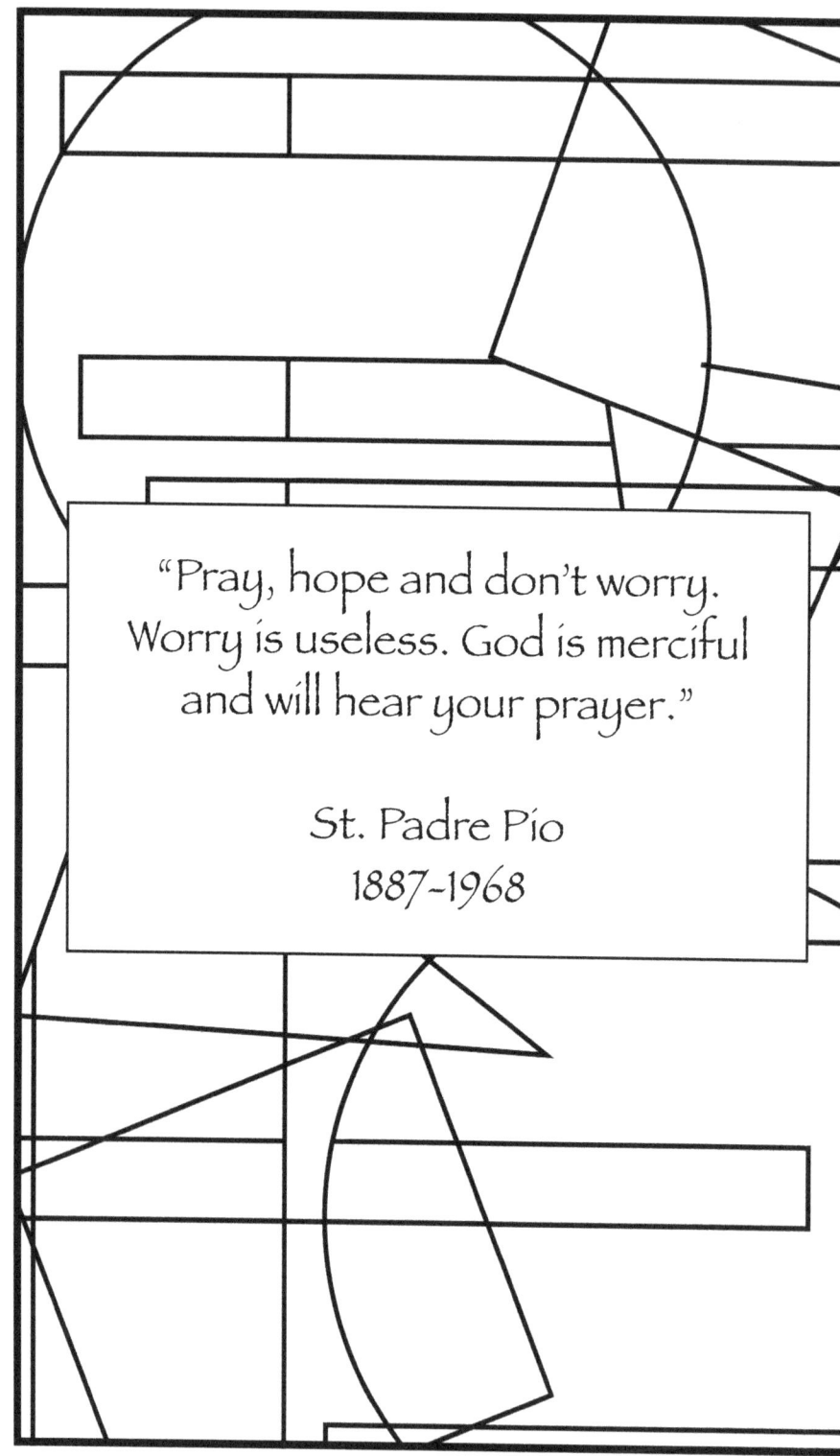

"Pray, hope and don't worry.
Worry is useless. God is merciful
and will hear your prayer."

St. Padre Pio
1887-1968

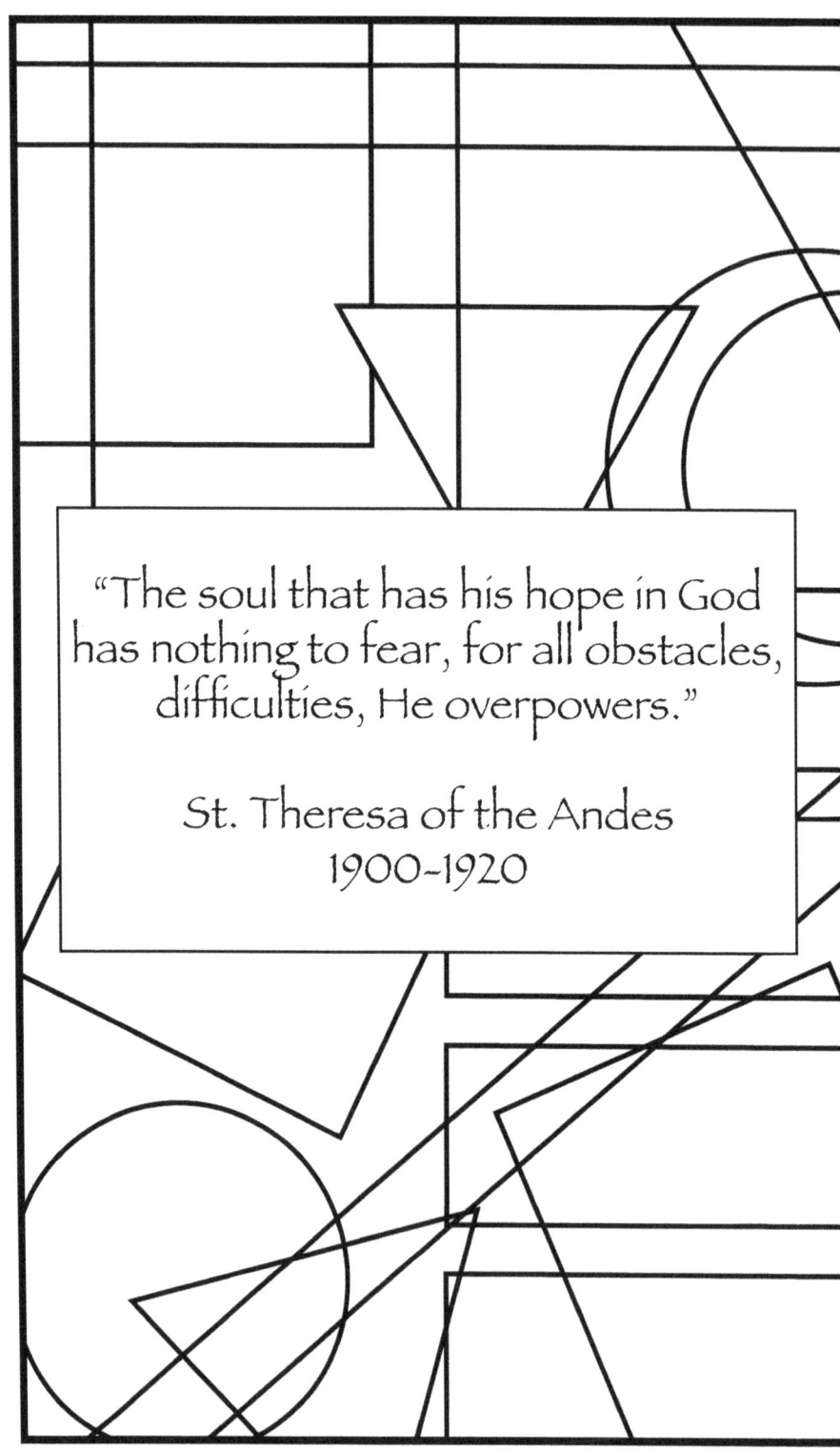

"The soul that has his hope in God
has nothing to fear, for all obstacles,
difficulties, He overpowers."

St. Theresa of the Andes
1900-1920

"I plead with you — never, ever give up on hope; never doubt, never tire and never become discouraged. Be not afraid."

St. Pope John Paul II
1920-2005

Also Available

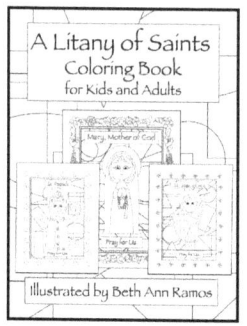

A Litany of Saints
Coloring Book
for Kids and Adults

Mary, Mother of God

Pray for Us

Illustrated by Beth Ann Ramos

SAINT SAYINGS
about
The Eucharist
A Picture Book for Catholic Kids

Illustrated by Beth Ann Ramos

SAINT SAYINGS
about
The Eucharist
A Coloring Book for Catholic Kids

Illustrated by Beth Ann Ramos

Free activities and coloring pages available at:
www.bethannramos.com/eucharist

Email books@bethannramos.com
to inquire about bulk or white label pricing for
your school, church, or diocese!

www.ingramcontent.com/pod-product-compliance
Lightning Source LLC
Chambersburg PA
CBHW051337120626
46547CB00016B/2590